Susan Stranks

PAPERPLAY

with Itsy and Bitsy

3

Illustrations and paper sculpture
by Norman Beardsley

Wolfe

Hello again! Here is the *third* book in our series and I hope you will all enjoy making the things in it as much as I did when we showed them on TV.

Don't forget, you can colour the pictures too.

Love from Susan

First published 1975 by Wolfe Publishing Limited, 10 Earlham Street, London WC2H 9LP

ISBN 0 7234 0696 0

This book is for Madeleine and Mark

A PAPERPLAY BOX

Find a big box, or an empty drawer, and put into it all the things you want to keep from being thrown out.

Here is a list of useful things to save.

Cardboard rolls and tubes	from	Paper towels and toilet paper
Cardboard boxes	"	Cereal, pet food and eggs
Cartons	"	Ice cream, yogurt, paper cups and plates
Tins	"	Mustard, syrup and drinking chocolate
Jars	"	Coffee, jam, pickles and savoury spread
Pictures	"	Magazines, comics, food packets and greetings cards

Other useful things

Corks, milk bottle tops, lolly sticks, string, buttons, used matches, hair pins, plastic aerosol tops, cotton reels, sequins and glitter.

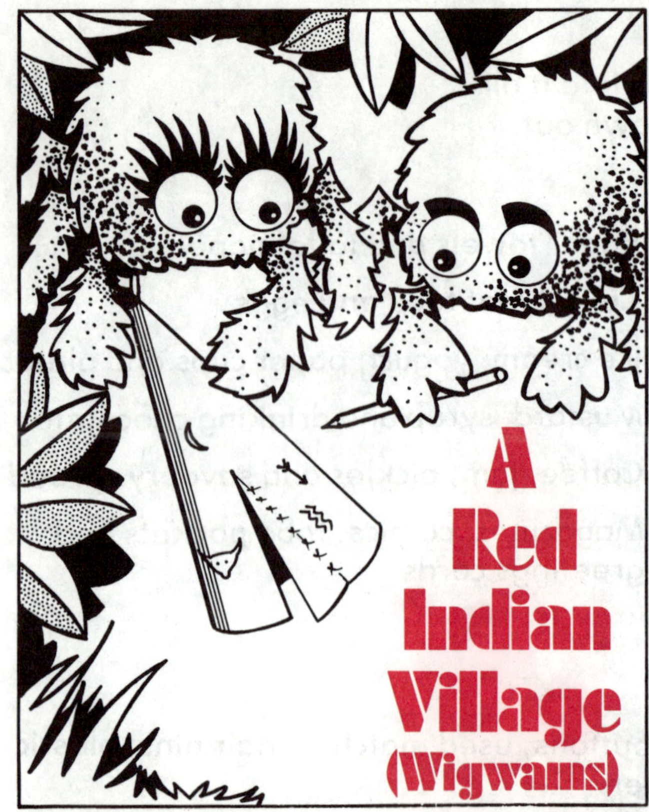

A Red Indian Village (Wigwams)

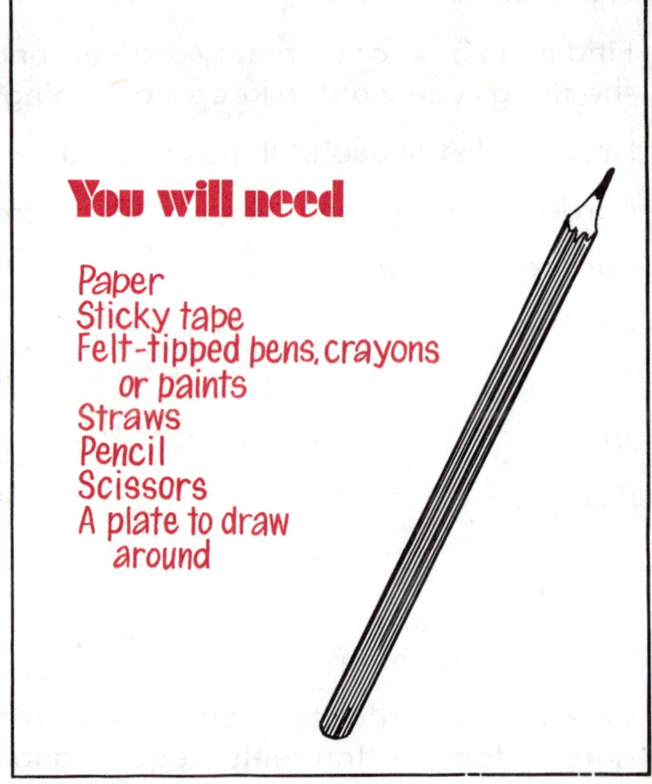

You will need

Paper
Sticky tape
Felt-tipped pens, crayons or paints
Straws
Pencil
Scissors
A plate to draw around

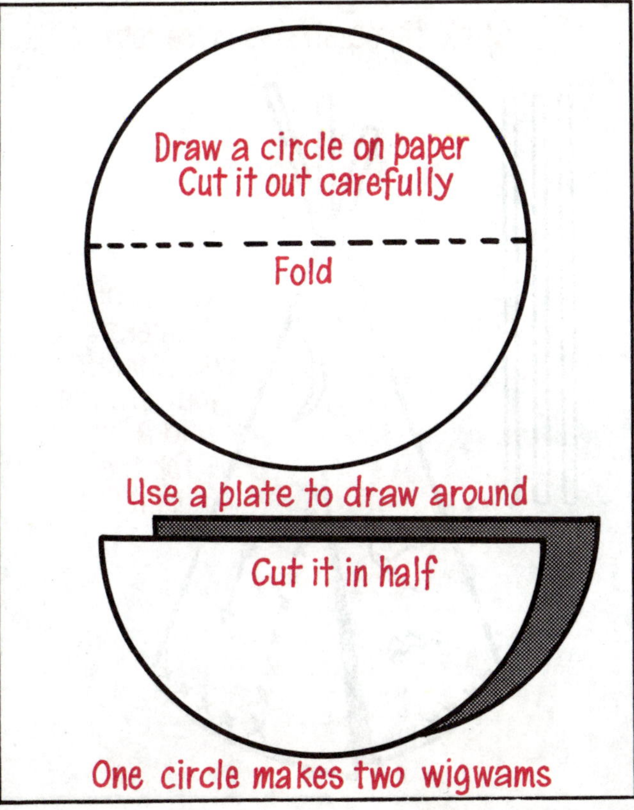
Draw a circle on paper
Cut it out carefully
Fold
Use a plate to draw around
Cut it in half
One circle makes two wigwams

Cut
Make a cut for the door and
decorate your wigwam.
Crosses look like stitching;
arrows and buffaloes are
good Indian pictures.
Fold back the door

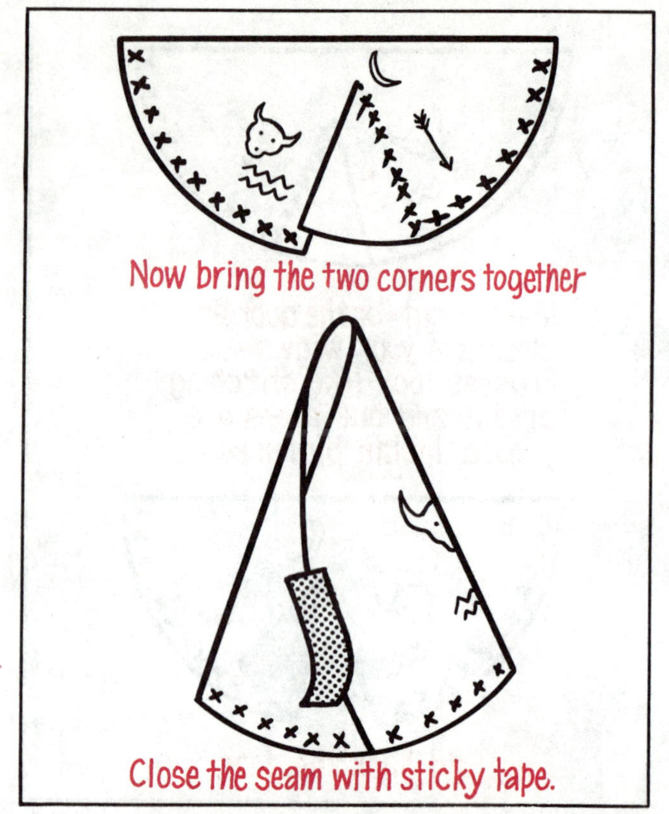
Now bring the two corners together
Close the seam with sticky tape.

Stick three straws in the top
Make lots of different wigwams for your village and a big one for the chief

A Totem Pole

In days gone by, every Indian village had a totem pole. These poles were hand-made out of tree trunks, with carvings of eagles and buffaloes and other animals on them. Sometimes they were painted bright colours. The American Indian people believed the totem pole helped to ward off evil spirits and keep their village safe.

What you need

Two cardboard rolls
Cardboard
Paint or stickers
Pencils
Scissors

Take two cardboard rolls the same size
Cut two slots in one
And four slots in the other
You can make your own rolls by rolling cardboard around a bottle and sticking down the seam with tape.

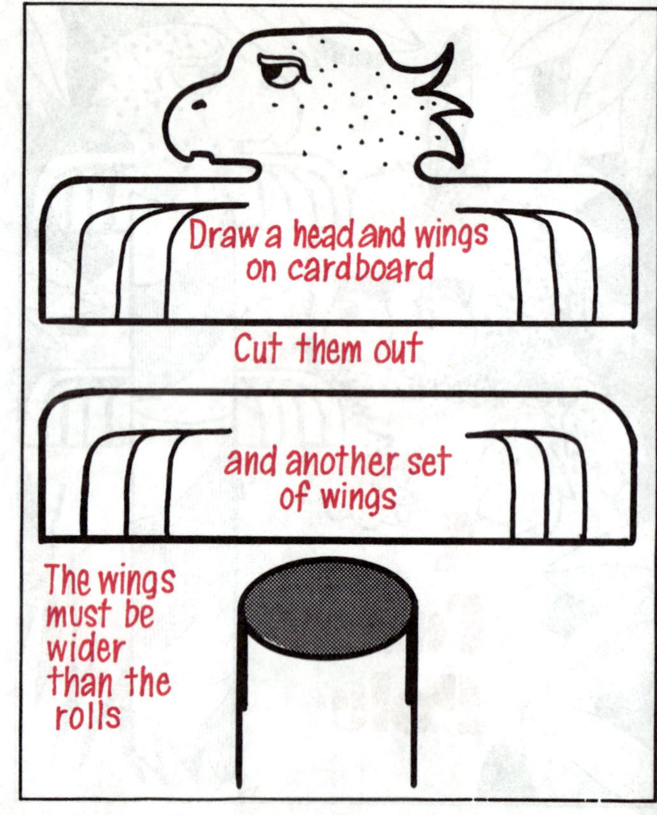
Draw a head and wings on cardboard
Cut them out
and another set of wings
The wings must be wider than the rolls

Now slot
the wings
between the
two rolls

And the
head on
top
Decorate your
totem pole
with paint or
stickers

Little Running Itsy
Smoke a peace pipe
Have a pow-wow
Big Chief Sitting Bitsy

Sweet smelling Flowers

You will need

Paper tissue hankies
Felt-tipped pens
Sticky tape
Twigs or ribbon
Scissors
A few drops of scent
Stickers
Stones
Plastic bottle
for the vase

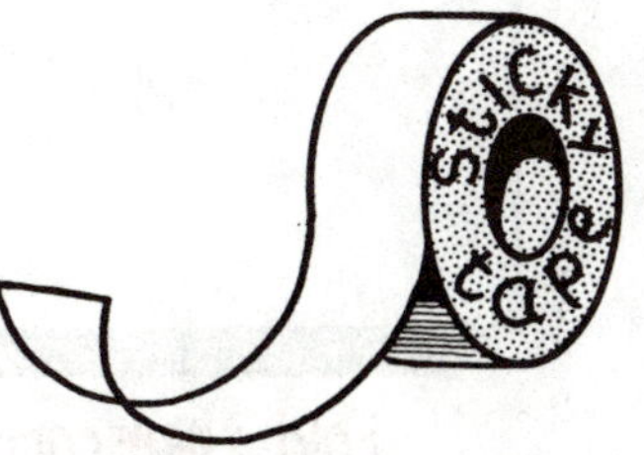

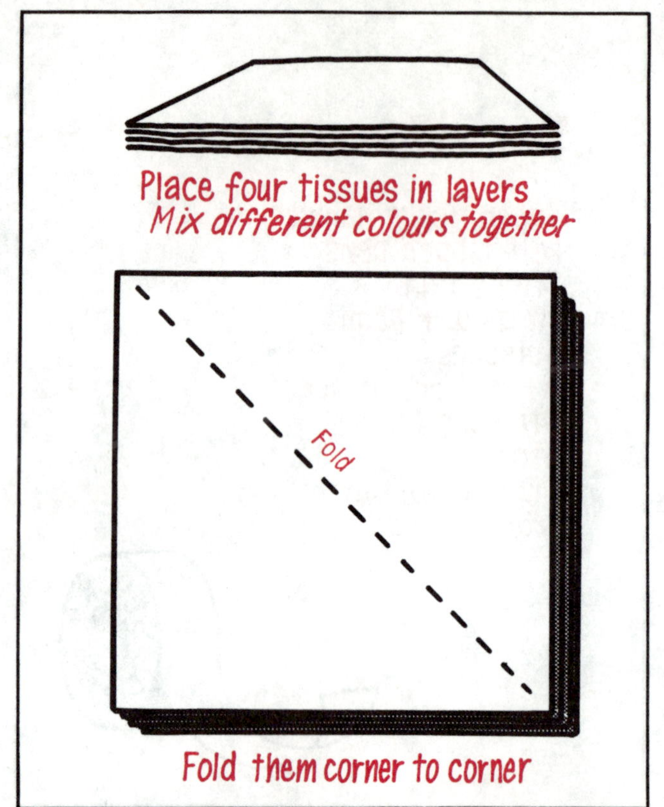
Place four tissues in layers
Mix different colours together
Fold
Fold them corner to corner

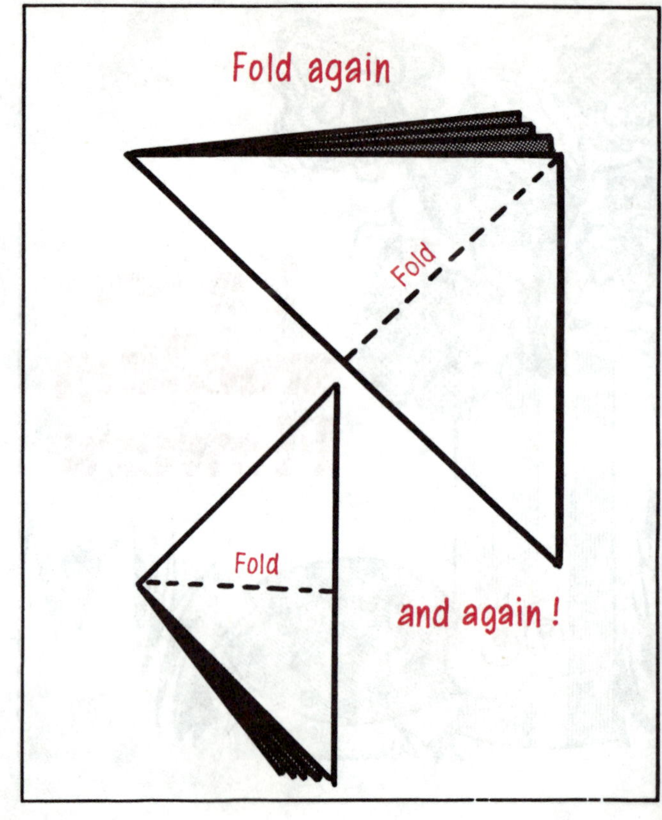
Fold again
Fold
Fold
and again !

Draw a petal shape and cut around it
Open out the flower shape

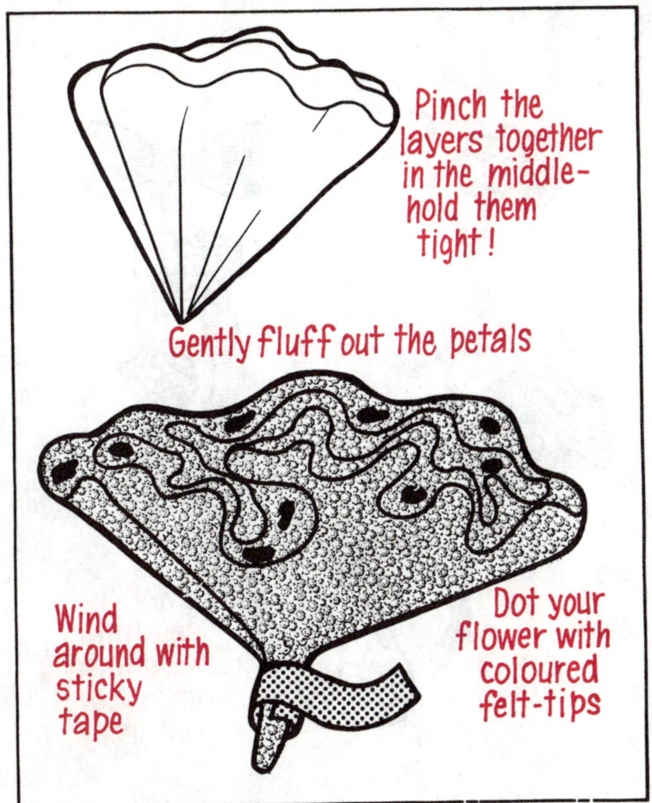
Pinch the layers together in the middle- hold them tight!
Gently fluff out the petals
Wind around with sticky tape
Dot your flower with coloured felt-tips

An easy vase for your blooms

Cardew's Monster

What you need

Two egg-box tops
Cardboard
Felt-tipped pens or paint
String
Glue
Scissors

Draw the monster's
head and neck,
cut it out
Draw the monster's
back, cut it out
Folded cardboard
Folded cardboard
Two egg-boxes ready for your monster

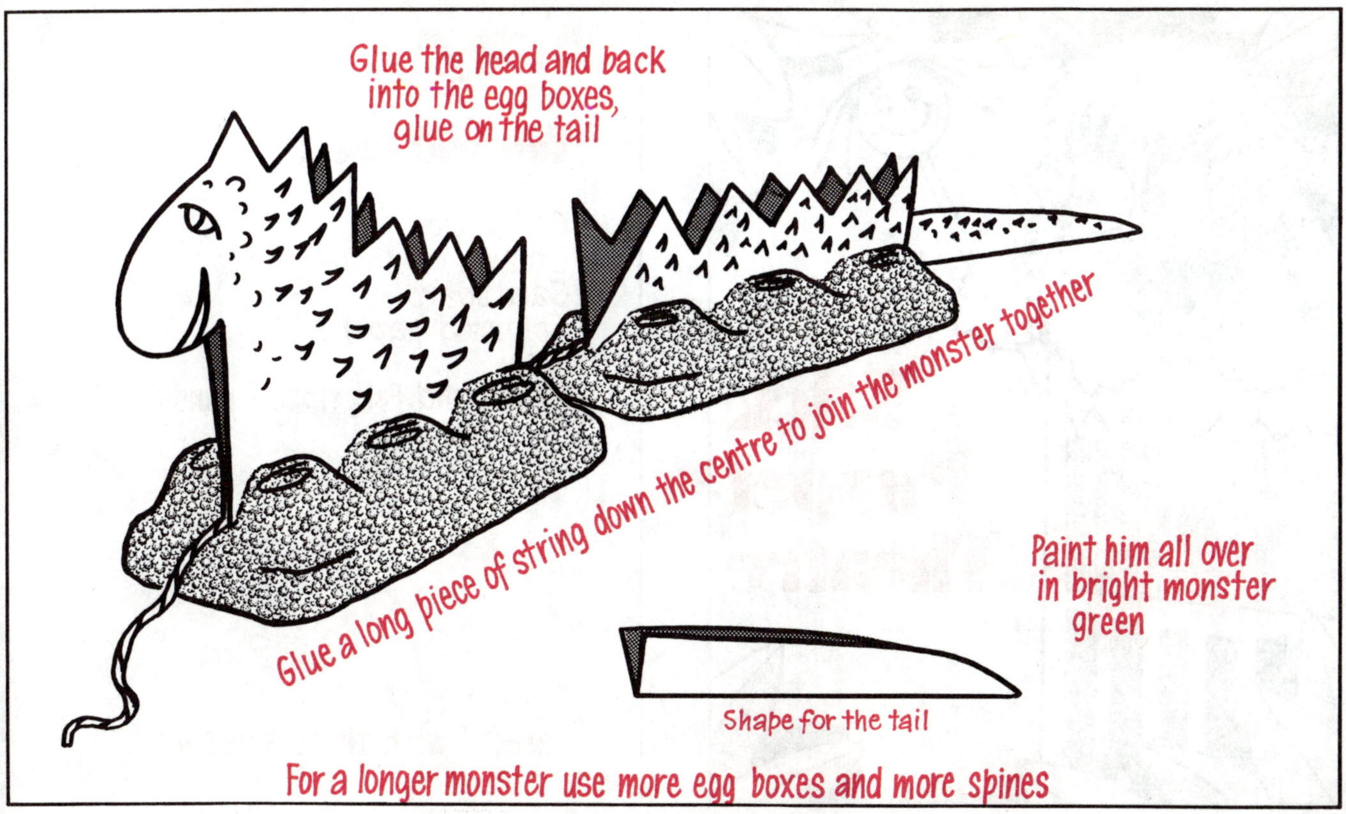
Glue the head and back
into the egg boxes,
glue on the tail
Glue a long piece of string down the centre to join the monster together
Paint him all over
in bright monster
green
Shape for the tail
For a longer monster use more egg boxes and more spines

Stick Puppet Theatre

You will need

Cereal box
Straws
Cardboard
Coloured paper
Wool
Paints and felt-tipped pens
Scissors

Careful with those scissors

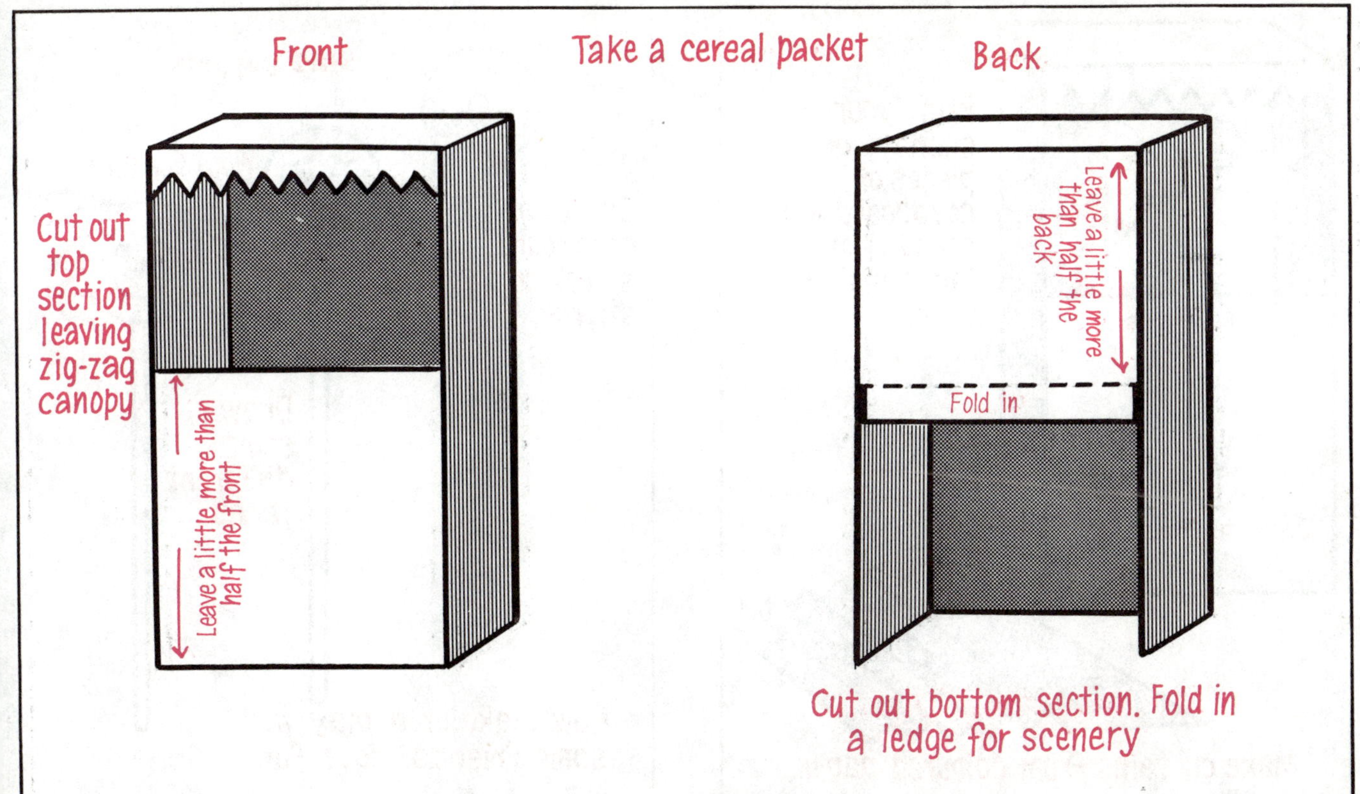
Front
Take a cereal packet
Back
Cut out top section leaving zig-zag canopy
Leave a little more than half the front
Leave a little more than half the back
Fold in
Cut out bottom section. Fold in a ledge for scenery

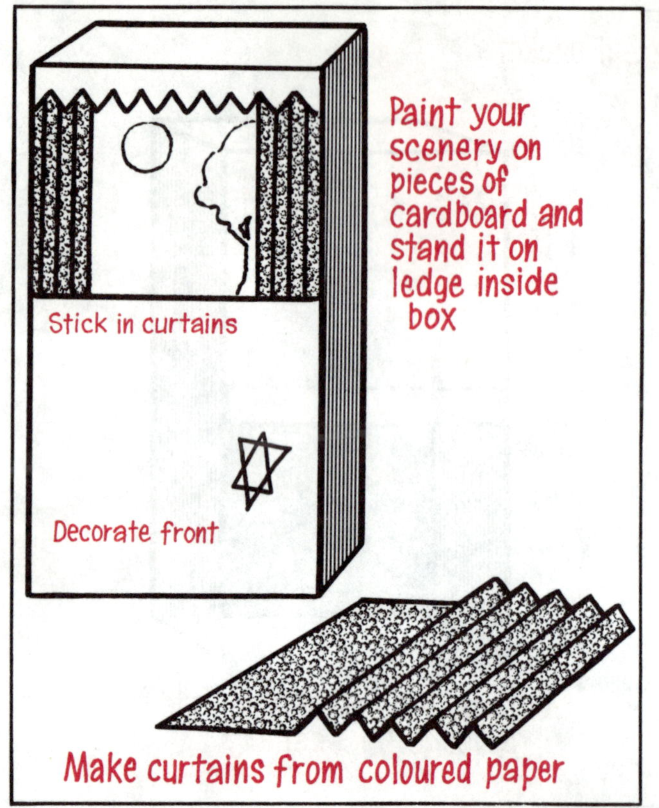
Paint your scenery on pieces of cardboard and stand it on ledge inside box
Stick in curtains
Decorate front
Make curtains from coloured paper

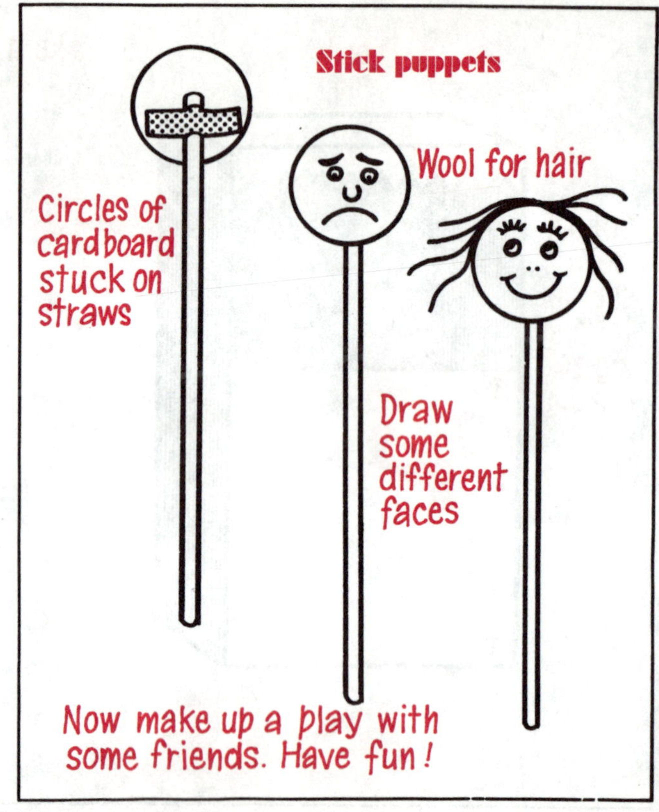
Stick puppets
Wool for hair
Circles of cardboard stuck on straws
Draw some different faces
Now make up a play with some friends. Have fun!

Look... Cardew and Boris are enjoying the play

Paper Butterflies for Kate

These butterflies look very pretty hanging from the ceiling, or you can stick them on twigs or stand them in a vase

What you need

Paper
Felt-tipped pens
Glitter or sequins *if you wish*
Scissors
Cotton

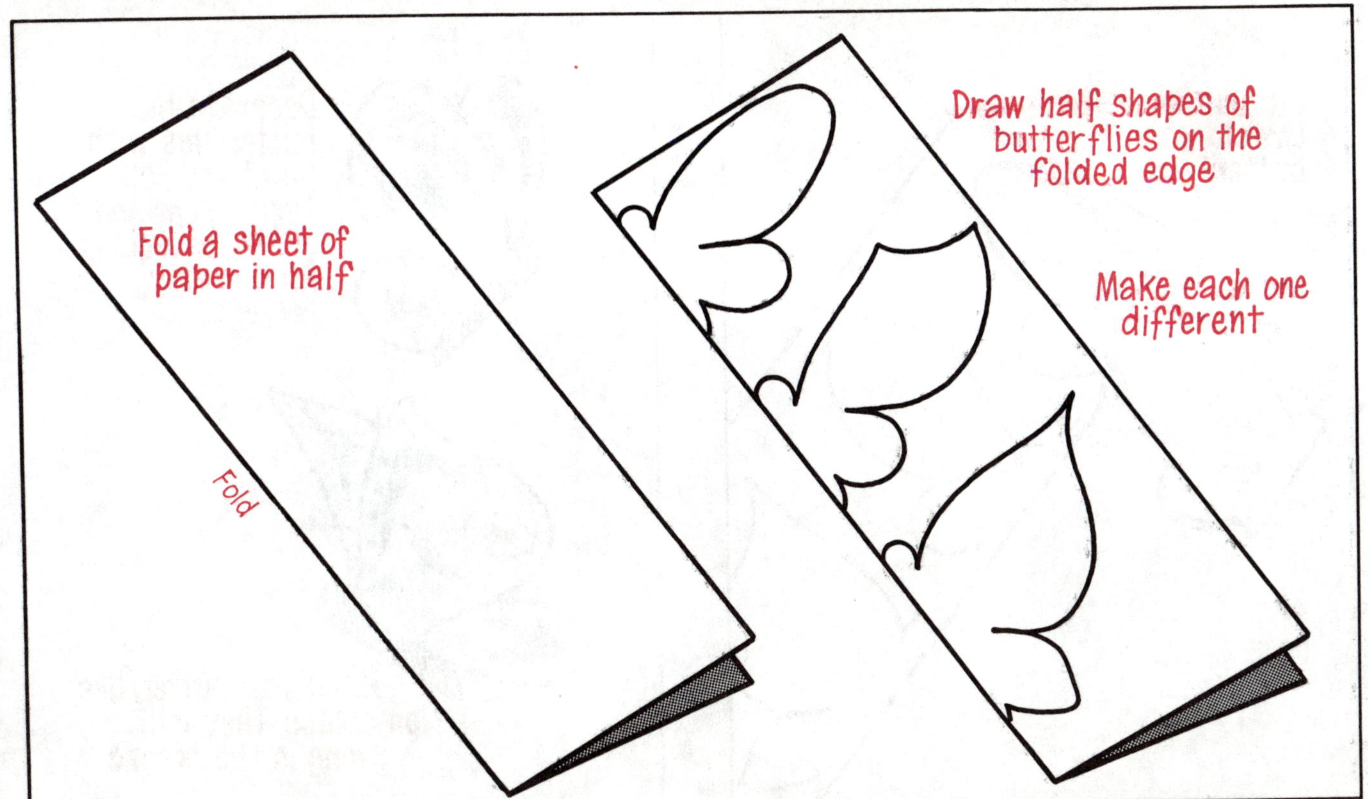
Fold a sheet of paper in half
Fold
Draw half shapes of butterflies on the folded edge
Make each one different

Cut out the shapes.
Unfold your
butterflies

Decorate the
butterflies with
paint and felt-
tipped pens. Add
glitter or sequins
for a pretty
effect
Hang your butterflies
on cotton. They will
swing in the breeze

The Normans or Northmen originally came from Scandinavia and settled in France hundreds of years ago. They came over and conquered England in 1066. They wore steel helmets and carried heavy swords when they went into battle and they must have looked very fierce indeed.

You will need

Cardboard
Sticky tape
Felt-tipped pens
Scissors
Foil *if you wish*

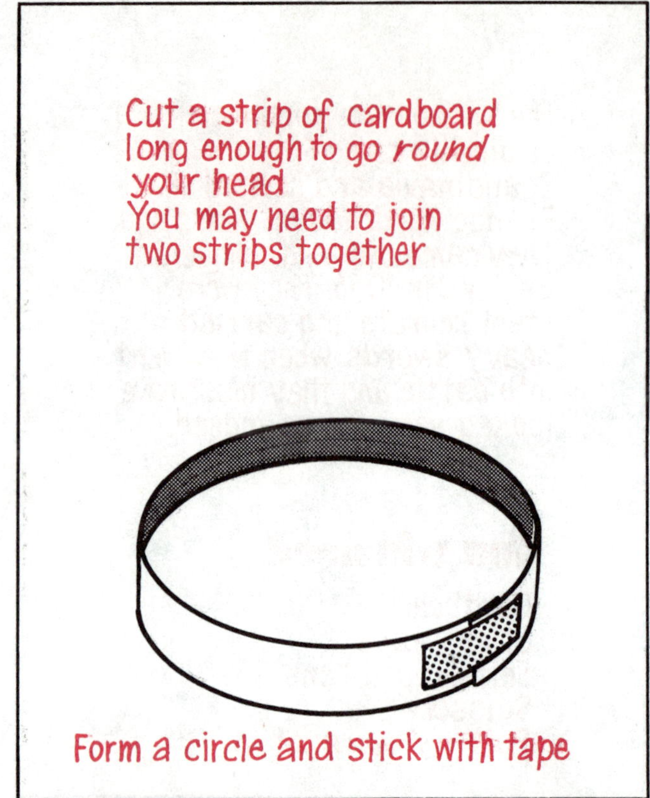
Cut a strip of cardboard
long enough to go *round*
your head
You may need to join
two strips together
Form a circle and stick with tape

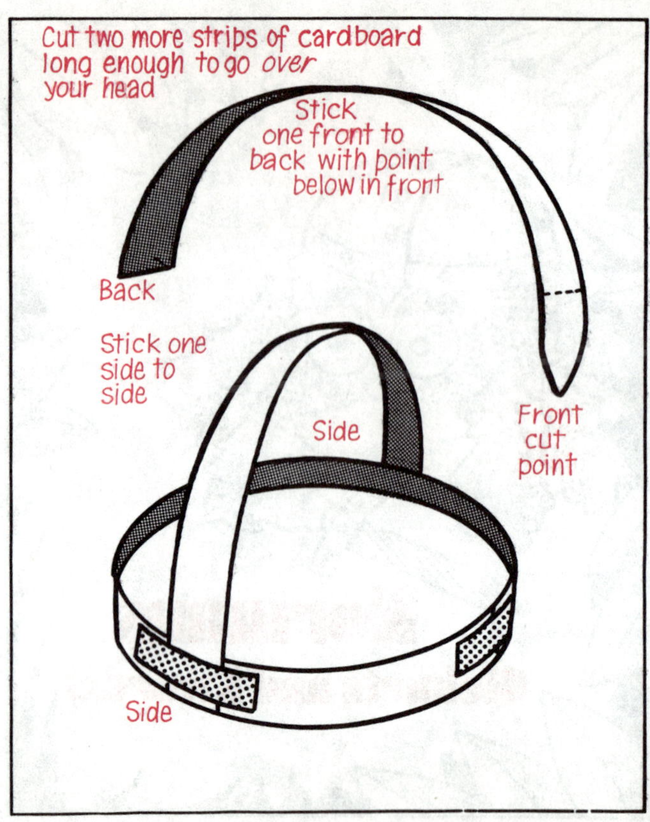
Cut two more strips of cardboard
long enough to go *over*
your head
Stick
one front to
back with point
below in front
Back
Stick one
side to
side
Side
Front
cut
point
Side

Now draw some rivets on your helmet
They will look shiny if you leave a speck of white on each

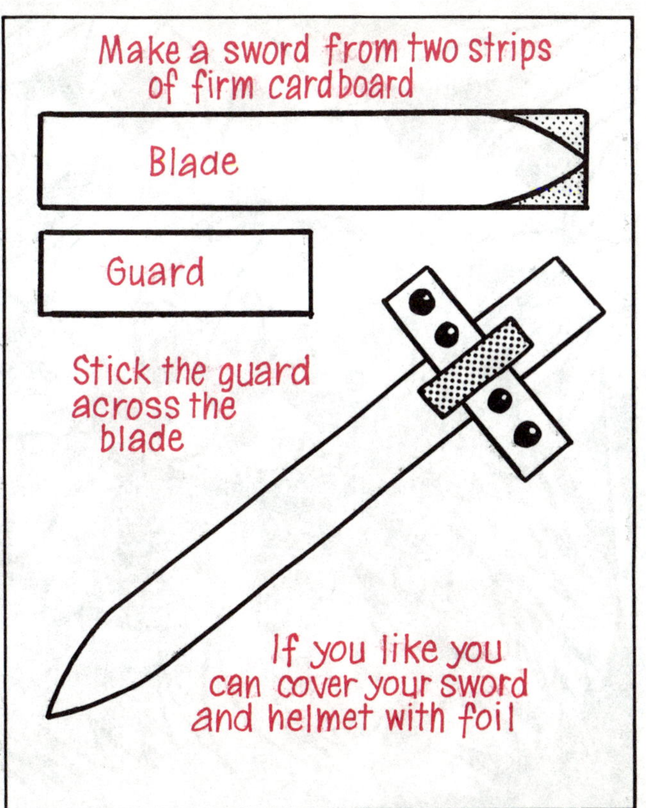
Make a sword from two strips of firm cardboard
Blade
Guard
Stick the guard across the blade
If you like you can cover your sword and helmet with foil

What you need

Washing-up liquid bottle
Cardboard
Straws
Felt-tipped pens or
stickers
Sticky tape or glue
Scissors

Follow the instructions carefully and you will be able to slide the three stages apart whenever you want to

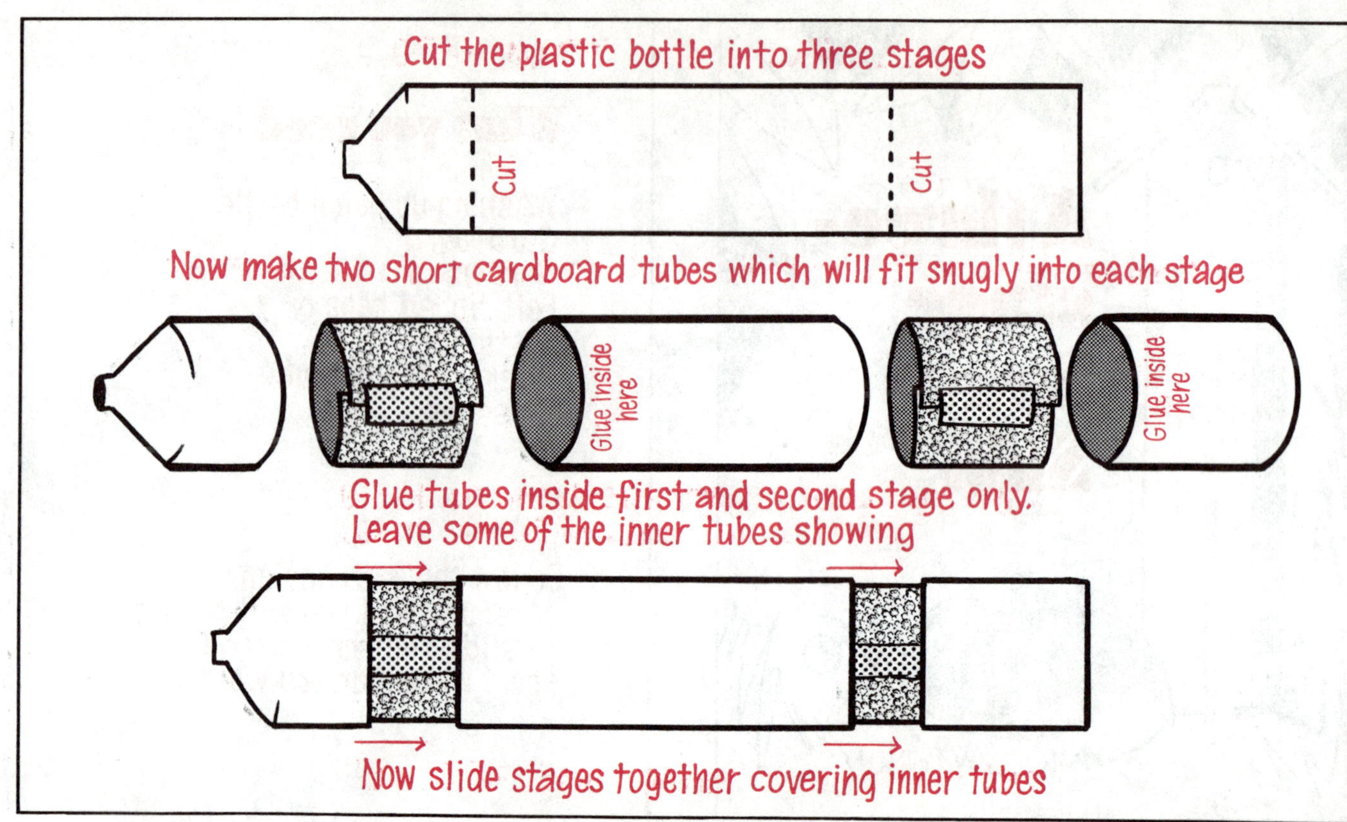
Cut the plastic bottle into three stages
Cut
Cut
Now make two short cardboard tubes which will fit snugly into each stage
Glue inside here
Glue inside here
Glue tubes inside first and second stage only.
Leave some of the inner tubes showing
Now slide stages together covering inner tubes

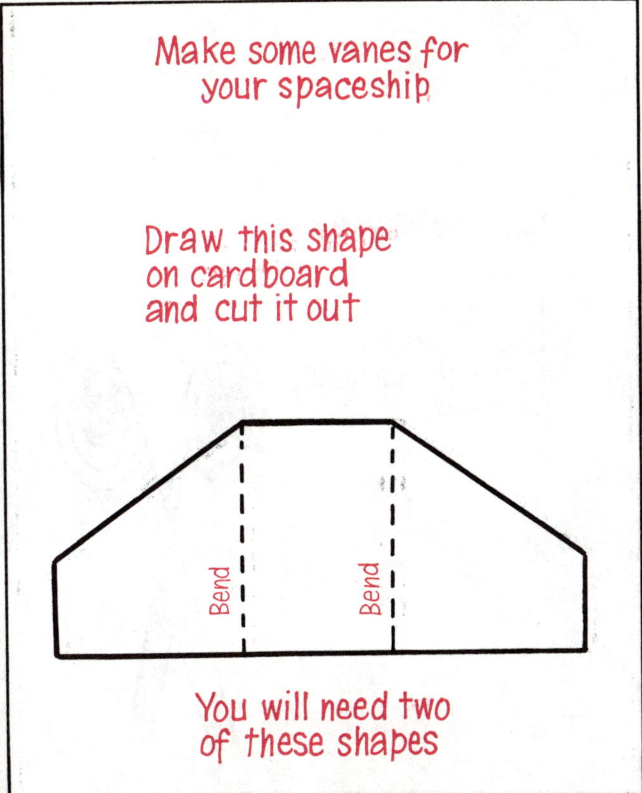
Make some vanes for your spaceship
Draw this shape on cardboard and cut it out
Bend
Bend
You will need two of these shapes

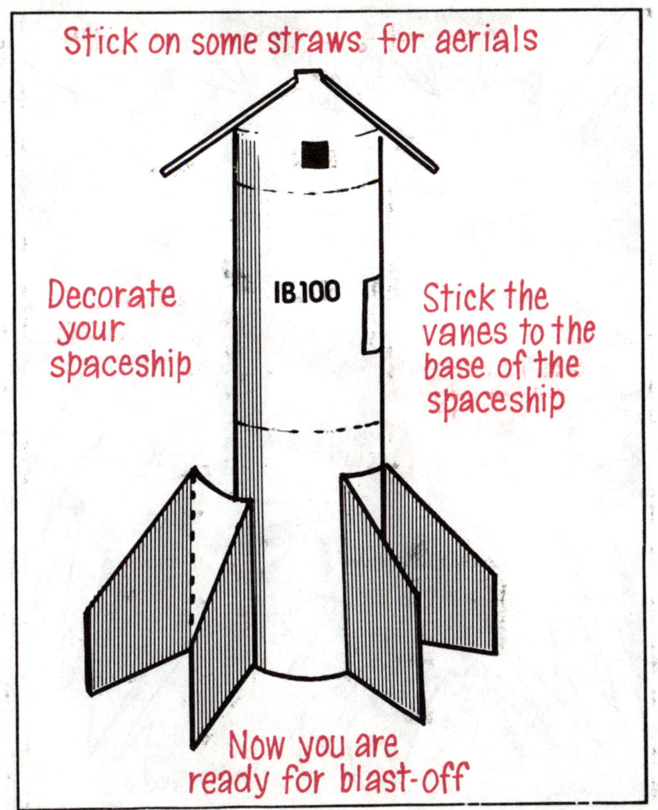
Stick on some straws for aerials
Decorate your spaceship
IB100
Stick the vanes to the base of the spaceship
Now you are ready for blast-off

You will need

Paper
Card board
Felt-tipped pens
Scissors

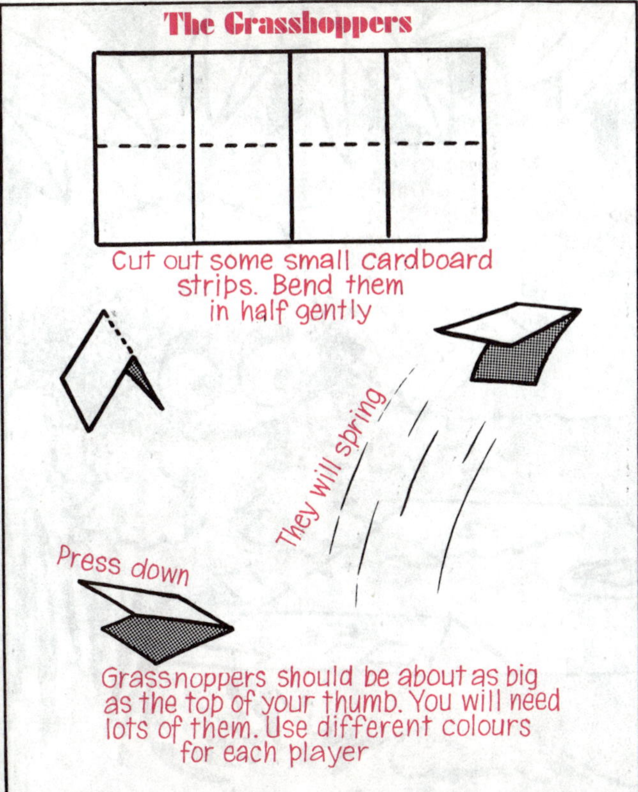
The Grasshoppers
Cut out some small cardboard strips. Bend them in half gently
They will spring
Press down
Grassnoppers should be about as big as the top of your thumb. You will need lots of them. Use different colours for each player

Flowers
1
4
2
Draw a plan of a garden
6
Number the areas 1 to 6
5
House
Trees
3

Give each player six grasshoppers, make sure they spring well...
Take turns to spring them from the table to the garden, then add up your scores. The highest is the winner
2
3
4
5

Paper Animals

What you need

Paper
Felt-tipped pens
Glue or paste
Scissors

Take a square of paper. Fold it in half corner to corner
Fold and cut
Now you have two triangles

Barney Bull
Take one triangle and roll the widest end under the pointed end
A little glue will hold it in place
Glue
Glue
Draw eyes and a nose for the bull

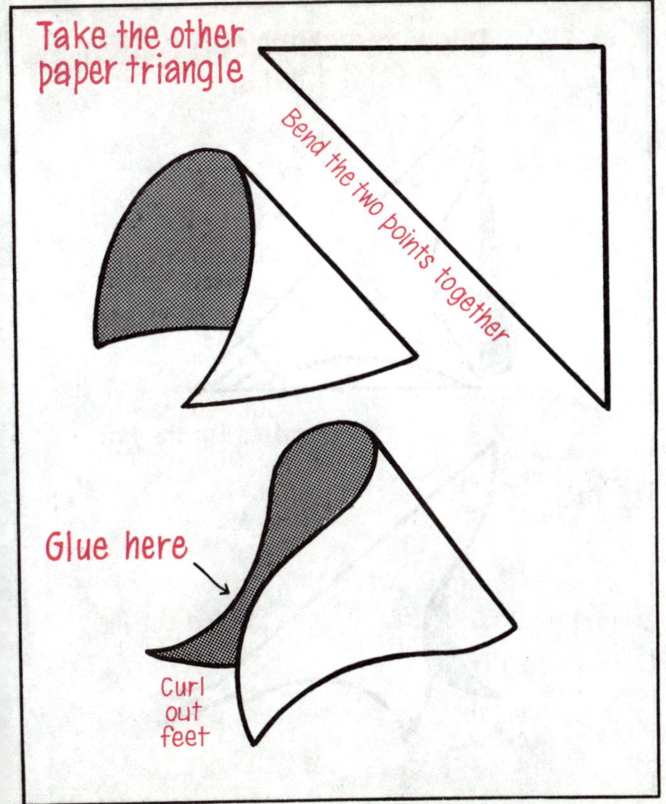
Take the other
paper triangle
Bend the two points together
Glue here
Curl
out
feet

Use very small dabs of glue
to stick the pieces together.
Be careful not
to crush him
Glue
Glue
Glue
Glue
Make a paper tail

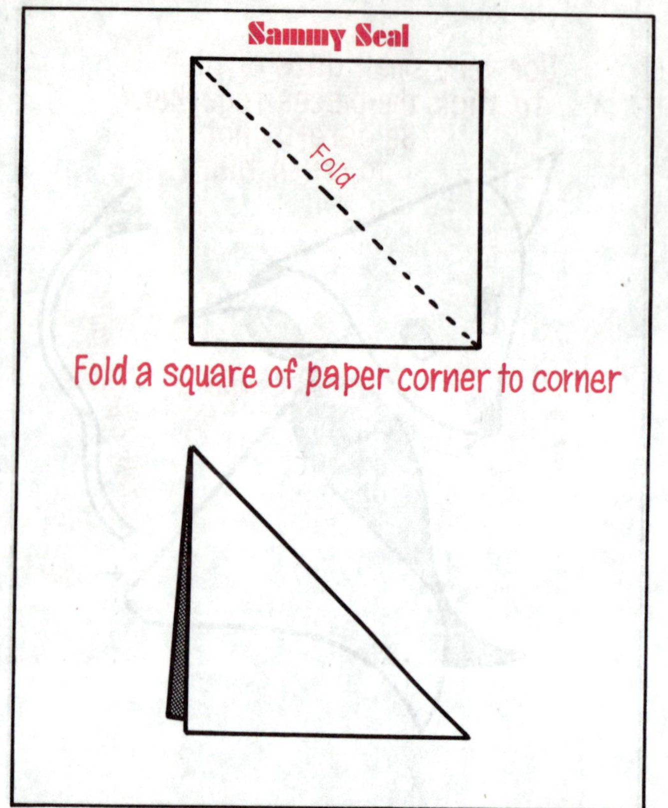
Sammy Seal
Fold
Fold a square of paper corner to corner

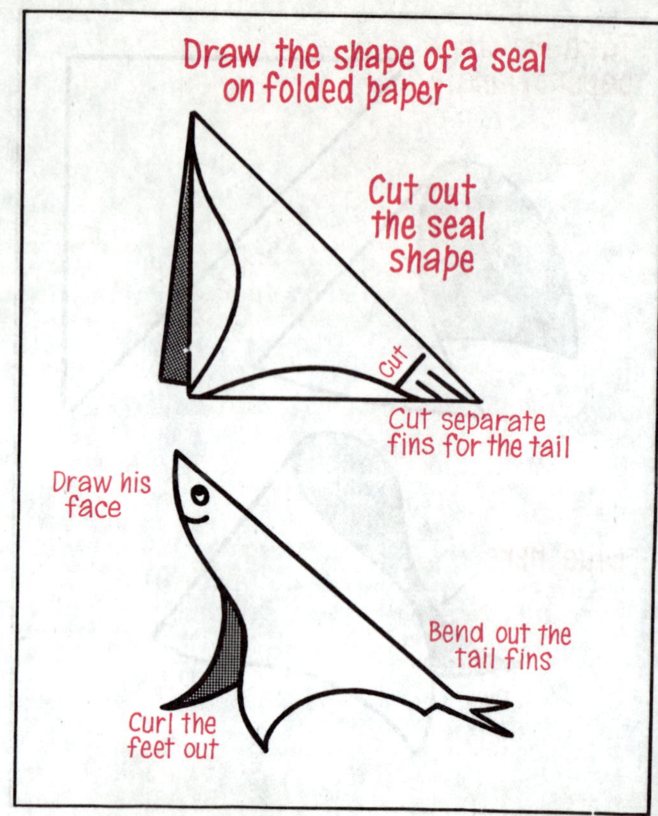
Draw the shape of a seal
on folded paper
Cut out
the seal
shape
Cut
Cut separate
fins for the tail
Draw his
face
Bend out the
tail fins
Curl the
feet out

You will need

Cardboard
String
Felt-tipped pens
Wool
Sticky tape
Scissors

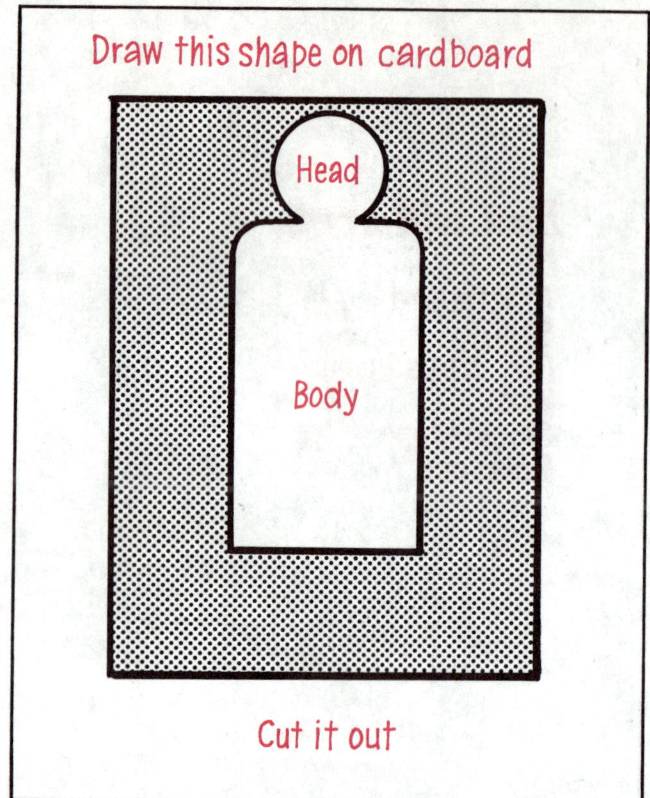
Draw this shape on cardboard
Head
Body
Cut it out

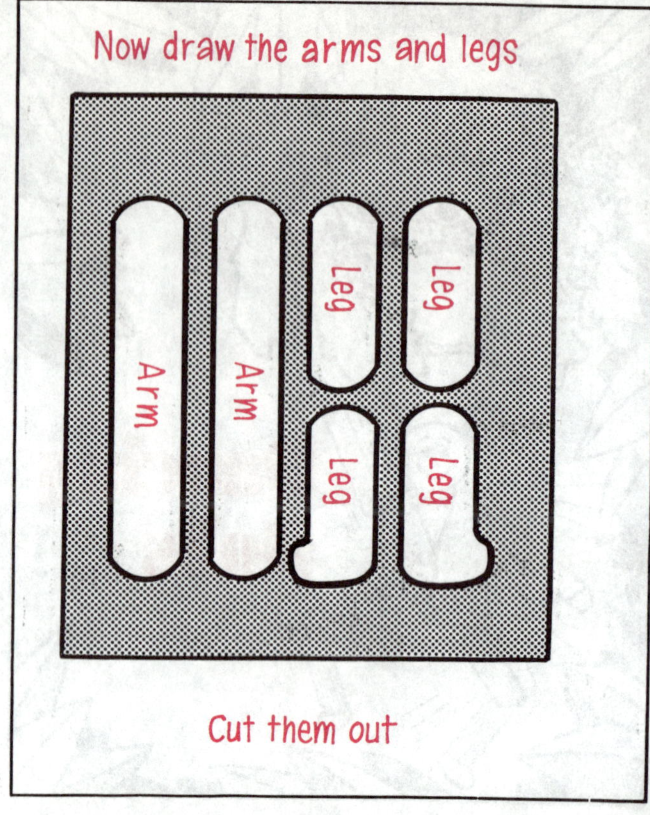
Now draw the arms and legs
Arm
Arm
Leg
Leg
Leg
Leg
Cut them out

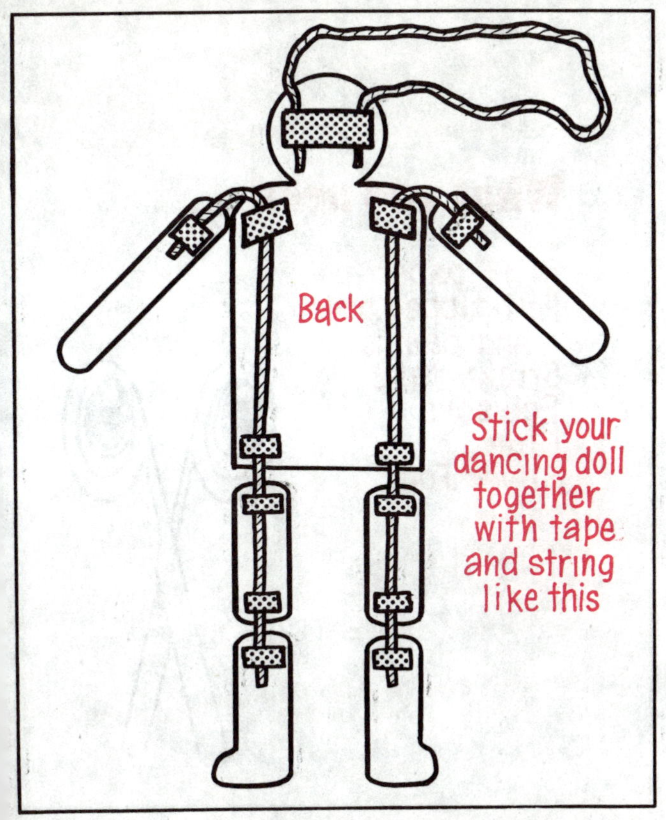
Back
Stick your dancing doll together with tape and string like this

Make a boy doll.... and a girl
Use wool for hair
See how they dance !

Paper Houses

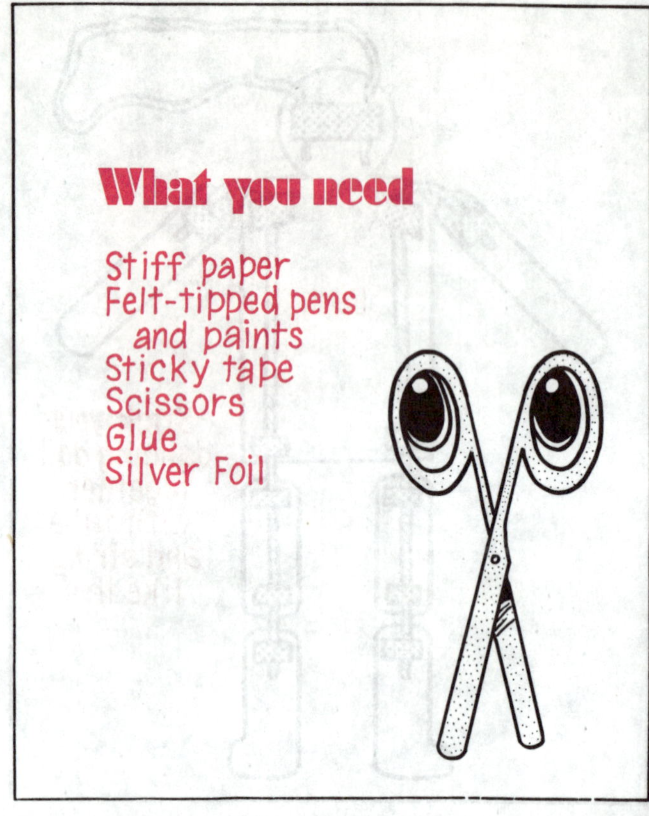

What you need

- Stiff paper
- Felt-tipped pens and paints
- Sticky tape
- Scissors
- Glue
- Silver Foil

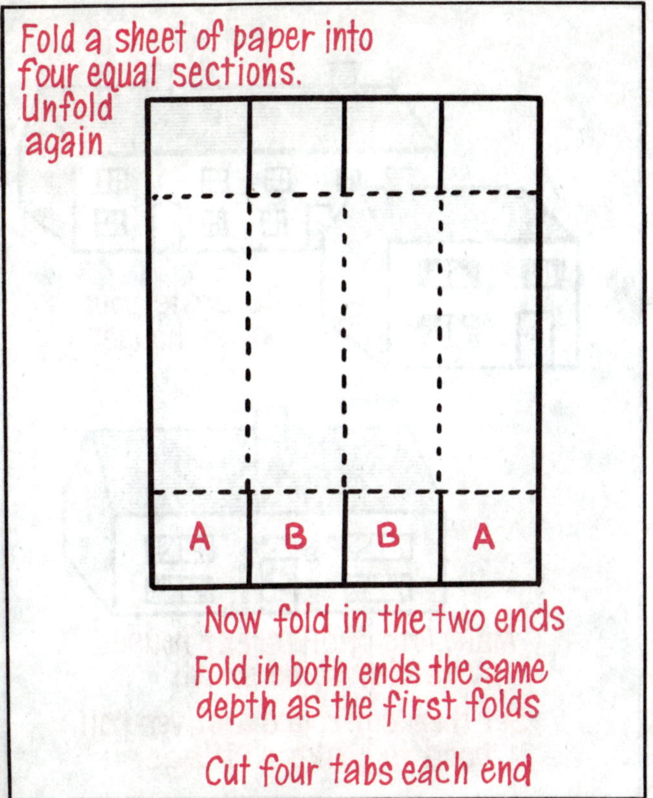
Fold a sheet of paper into four equal sections. Unfold again
A
B
B
A
Now fold in the two ends
Fold in both ends the same depth as the first folds
Cut four tabs each end

B
B
A
A
Glue
Do this at both ends to form your house. Stick with glue

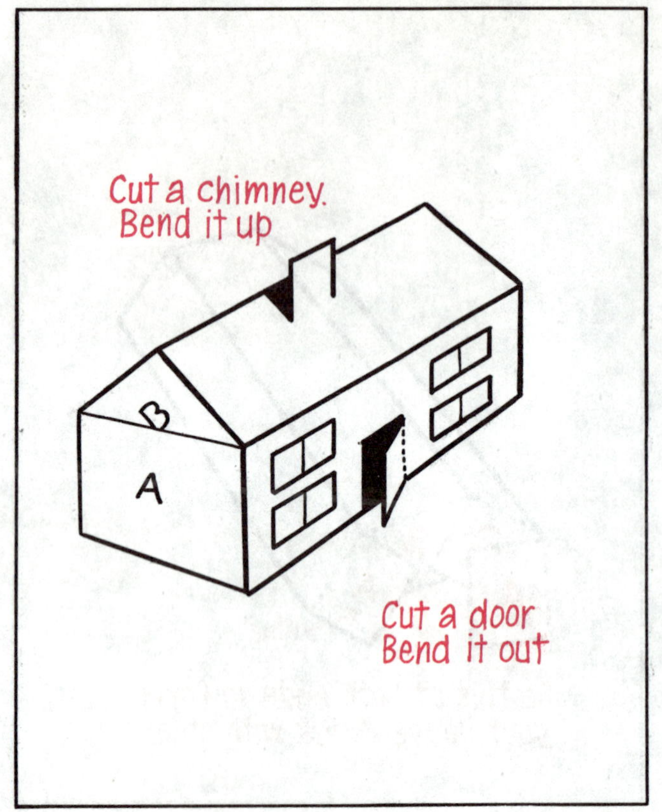
Cut a chimney.
Bend it up
B
A
Cut a door
Bend it out

Decorate your
paper houses
Make lots of different houses,
some big, some small
Set them out round a silver-foil
pond to make a village

You will need

Paper
Sticky tape
String
Scissors

Paper Lanterns

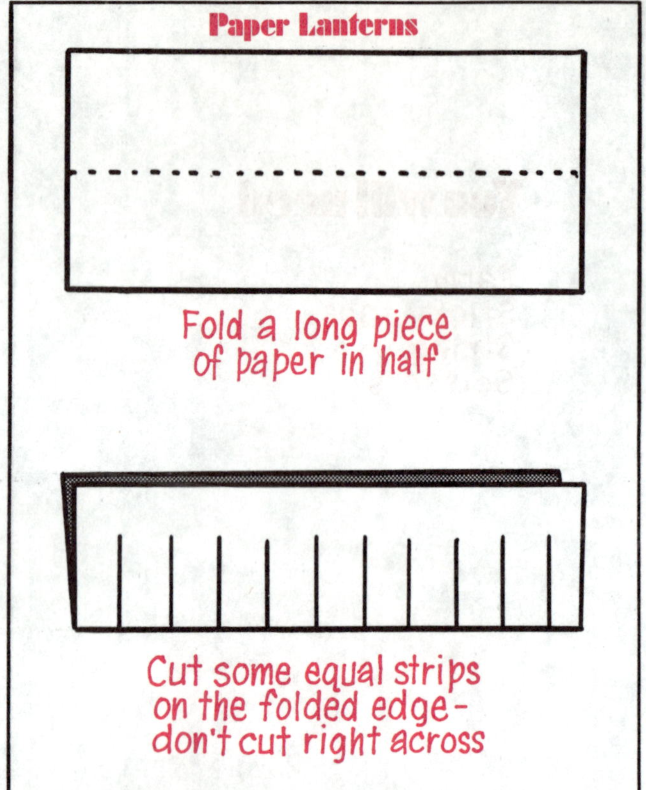

Mystery Masks
Fold a large piece of paper in half
Cut fringe for hair
cut
Draw a face on the folded edge
Cut it out

Bend nose outwards
Tie on with string
Make different masks for each of your friends.
Paper plates and cups mean no washing up.
Have a lovely party

Printed by Eyre & Spottiswoode Ltd at Grosvenor Press Portsmouth